PIANO SEASCAPES

12 original piano pieces inspired by the sea

PAM WEDGWOOD

FABER *ff* MUSIC

INTRODUCTION

Recently, I moved house to live near the sea. This is something that I had always promised myself I would do in the coda section of my life. The move has proved to be a wonderful inspiration to compose evocative and descriptive pieces based on some of my favourite seascape paintings. In this collection I have tried to give each piece my own interpretation of the artwork with strong melody lines and imaginative settings. I do hope you will enjoy playing all the pieces and you feel inspired by the art collection. Relax and enjoy!

Pam Wedgwood

© 2019 by Faber Music Ltd
This edition first published in 2019
Bloomsbury House
74–77 Great Russell Street
London WC1B 3DA
Music processed by Jackie Leigh
Cover design by Chloë Alexander
Cover image: *On the Beach*, Boudin (Chester Dale Collection)
Printed in England by Caligraving Ltd
All rights reserved

ISBN10: 0-571-54106-2
EAN13: 978-0-571-54106-5

To buy Faber Music publications or to find out about the full range of titles available
please contact your local music retailer or Faber Music sales enquiries:

Faber Music Ltd, Burnt Mill, Elizabeth Way, Harlow CM20 2HX
Tel: +44 (0) 1279 82 89 82   Fax: +44 (0) 1279 82 89 83
sales@fabermusic.com   fabermusicstore.com

CONTENTS

Victoria and Albert

"On the Beach" (Boudin)

Pam Wedgwood

Queen Victoria and Prince Albert spent a lot of time at Osborne House on the Isle of Wight. This painting depicts the pair on a day at the beach, presenting a very Victorian scene. Play this piece with a relaxed and joyful feel.

"Those who live by the sea can hardly form a single thought of which the sea would not be part." — Hermann Broch

Seascapes

"Cliffs at Pourville" (Monet)

Pam Wedgwood

This beautiful painting by Monet gives me a great feeling of calm. It inspired me to write this relaxed, thoughtful melody.
Make sure to really bring the melody out and imagine that you are walking in this beautiful coastal scene.

"May your joys be as deep as the ocean's, / Your troubles as light as its foam.
And may you find sweet piece of mind / Wherever you may roam." — An Irish Blessing

All Washed Up
"Boats on a Beach, Eretat" (Courbet)

Pam Wedgwood

My inspiration for this painting came from the sadness I always feel when I see a neglected boat waiting on the beach to be loved by someone. The theme of this piece was composed while I was walking by the sea. Play this with a strong swing feel but not too fast. Think of it in a blues style; a little melancholic.

"Watch the little things, / A small leak will sink a great ship" — Benjamin Franklin

Slower
Tide going out!

Bathing Machines
"Victorian Bathing Machine" (Rheaume)

Pam Wedgwood

This painting gives us a real glimpse of a Victorian seascape. The bathing machine was described as a four-wheeled carriage covered with canvas in which one end is let down so that the bather can get into the water without being seen. A Victorian mobile changing room – what fun! Play this with a strong swing rhythm and enjoy.

"A little sea bathing would set me up forever." — Jane Austen

Moonlight Bossa

"Lighthouse" (Getty images)

Pam Wedgwood

This piece was inspired by the unique colours used in this vibrant painting. The piece is written in a
bossa nova style so play it in a bright and breezy way with lots of energy.

"How sweet the moonlight sleeps upon this bank! / Here will we sit and let the sounds of music
Creep in our ears: soft stillness and the night / Become the touches of sweet harmony." — William Shakespeare

Crystal Waters

"Dreamy Woman" (Olgaosa)

Pam Wedgwood

I love the colours in this painting, particularly those used for the woman's hat. What is she thinking about?
There is nothing better than having the time to sit and stare into the ocean; it's very therapeutic.
Play this calmly with oodles of thought.

*"…the monotonous fall of the waves on the beach, which for the most part beat a measured and soothing
tattoo to her thoughts seemed consolingly to repeat over and over again…"* — Virginia Woolf

Calmly with thought (♩. = 52)

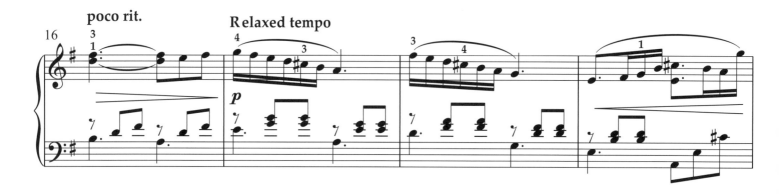

Sunset

"Sunset Over a Pond" (Ravier)

Pam Wedgwood

In this romantic watercolour the explosion of colours is mesmerising. The more you look, the more you see.
Play this with freedom and make it your own performance.

"The sea appears all golden / Beneath the sun-lit sky." — Heinrich Heine

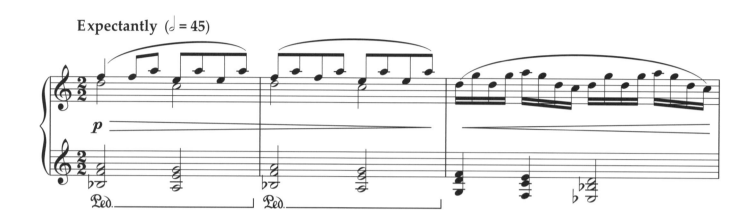

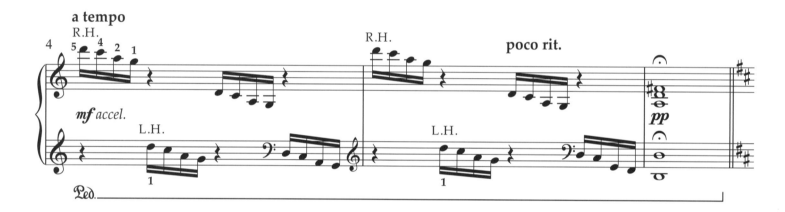

PIANO SEASCAPES

1 **On the Beach** (Eugene Boudin) "Victoria and Albert"
Chester Dale Collection

2 **Cliffs at Pourville** (Claude Monet) "Seascapes"
Collection of Mr. and Mrs. Mellon

3 **Boats on a Beach, Eretat** (Gustave Courbet) "All Washed Up"
Gift of the W. Averell Harriman Foundation in memory of Marie N. Harriman

4 **Victorian Bathing Machine** (Dave Rheaume) "Bathing Machines"
Dave Rheaume Artist

5 **Lighthouse** "Moonlight Bossa"
borojoint (Getty Images)

6 **Dreamy Woman** "Crystal Waters"
Olgaosa (Getty Images)

7 **Sunset Over a Pond** (François-Auguste Ravier) "Sunset"
Purchased as a Gift in Memory of Melvin R. Seiden

8 **Revere Beach** (Maurice Brazil Prendergast) "On the Rocks"
Collection of Mr. and Mrs. Paul Mellon

9 **Ground Swell** (Edward Hopper) "Messing About in a Boat"
Corcoran Collection (Museum Purchase, William A. Clark Fund)

10 **Regatta at Argenteuil** (Auguste Renoir) "The Regatta"
Ailsa Mellon Bruce Collection

11 **Skiffs** (Gustave Caillebotte) "Drifting By"
Collection of Mr. and Mrs. Paul Mellon

12 **The Much Resounding Sea** (Thomas Moran) "Stormy Seas"
Gift of the Avalon Foundation

7

8

Prendergast

9

11

10

12

On the Rocks

"Revere Beach" (Prendergast)

Pam Wedgwood

I had enormous fun writing this piece and I hope you will find the humour that runs through it.
The picture conjures up a fun day out at the sea, rambling across the rocks, picnics, and having an adventure
away from normal life. Play this with a light-hearted spirit and enjoy all the time changes.

"Our memories of the ocean will linger on, long after our footprints in the sand are gone." — Anonymous

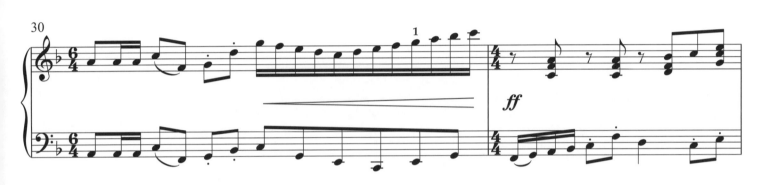

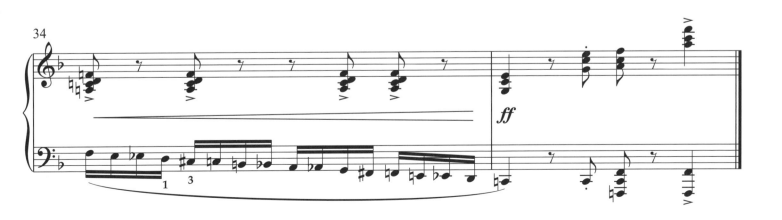

Messing About in a Boat

"Ground Swell" (Hopper)

Pam Wedgwood

This Hopper painting is one of my favourites. The blue sky, the rolling sea and relaxed figures on the boat offer
a sense of calm and serenity. It inspired me to write a relaxed, fun and swinging piece that mimics
the rocking and splashing of a bunch of friends messing about in a boat.

"There's nothing – absolutely nothing – half so much worth doing as simply messing about in boats." — Kenneth Grahame

The Regatta

"Regatta at Argenteuil" (Renoir)

Pam Wedgwood

This wonderful oil painting by Renoir really inspired me to shape the music around the painting –
there are so many different emotions to capture and I have used my own personal interpretation on how I see it.
Play this in a very relaxed mood. When you get to the swing section, make sure to emphasise the contrast.

"The days pass happily with me wherever my ship sails." — Joshua Slocum

Drifting By

"Skiffs" (Caillebotte)

Pam Wedgwood

This wonderful impressionist painting suggests a great feeling of relaxation, slowly drifting along with the flow of the water. Take your time with this and observe how the character of the piece changes at bar 21. Play peacefully and in a romantic style.

"Let your boat of life be light, packed with only what you need…" — Jerome K. Jerome

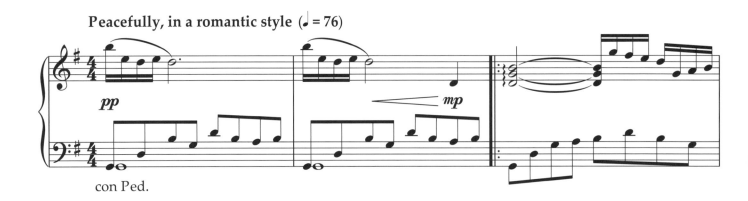

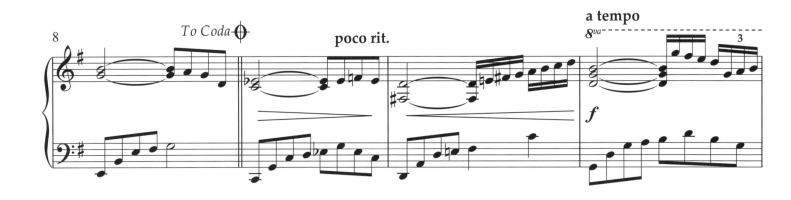

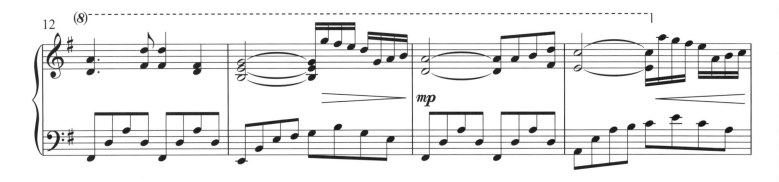

Stormy Seas
"The Much Resounding Sea" (Moran)

Pam Wedgwood

This atmospheric oil painting by Thomas Moran was the inspiration for my duet. I have tried to write each section so that it represents the changing moods and colours that happen during a storm. Play with complete conviction!

"The roaring of lions, the howling of wolves, the raging of the stormy sea, and the destructive sword, are portions of eternity, too great for the eye of man." — William Blake